PRODIGAL

Also by
Francine Marie Tolf

Rain, Lilies, Luck
Joliet Girl
Windy City Fragments
Like Saul
Blue-flowered Sundress

Prodigal

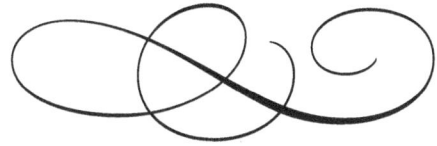

Poems by
Francine Marie Tolf

PINYON PUBLISHING
Montrose, Colorado

Copyright © 2012 by Francine Marie Tolf

All rights reserved. Except as permitted under the U.S. Copyright Act of 1976, no part of this publication may be reproduced, distributed, or transmitted in any form or by any means, or stored in a database or retrieval system, without the prior written permission of the publisher, except for brief quotations in articles, books, and reviews.

Book and Cover Design by Susan E. Elliott

Photograph of Francine Marie Tolf by Marc Marcovitz

First Edition: April 2012

Pinyon Publishing
23847 V66 Trail, Montrose, CO 81403
www.pinyon-publishing.com

Library of Congress Control Number: 2012934041
ISBN: 978-1-936671-08-3

Acknowledgments

Calliope: Wild Swan of Nimes

The Christian Century: Meeting Sophia

Dust and Fire: Helen, In Their Company, Wednesday

Green Hills Literary Lantern: Meadow Lilies

Isotope: Between You and Me

Main Channel Voices: Almost a Happy Poem, Magnolia, The Neighbor's Dog

Nimrod: Sky, Tonight

Parva Sed Apta: Two Experiments and an Aside

Plainsongs: Three Dreams in Three Colors

Poetry U.S.A. (Mother Earth): First Step, Small News Item

Prairie Winds: They Have Healed

Rockford Review: Kinship

Santa Fe Review: Last Day in North Woods

Spoon River Poetry Review: Cana, Veal Calf

Water-Stone: An Easter Poem for Christopher Smart, Poetry Remembers

White Pelican Review: Cottonwoods, Migration

A number of poems in this book appeared in *Like Saul*, a chapbook published by Plan B Press in 2008.

"Small News Item in the Midst of War" and "Seel" were reprinted in the 2011 issue of *Written River*.

I am deeply grateful to Blacklock Nature Sanctuary, the Barbara Deming/Money for Women Foundation, the Minnesota State Arts Board, and the Elizabeth George Foundation. Their grants allowed me the time to work on and complete this collection.

Contents

Sky 1
Naming 2
Poetry Remembers 3
An Easter Poem for Christopher Smart 4
She only wants to write 6
Two Experiments and an Aside 7
Red-tailed Fox 8
First Day at Blacklock Nature Sanctuary 9
Migration 10
Wild Swan of Nimes 11
In This Rain 12
Taking the Master's Hand 13
Someone is beating a woman 14
seel: to stitch closed the eyes (of a falcon) during training 15
Chinese Seahorse 16
Cottonwoods 17
Last Day at North Woods 18
Don't Disappoint Them 19
First Step 20
Meeting Sophia 21
Great, grey / sisterly shape 22
A Good Thing 23
On Washington Avenue Bridge 24
Her Heaven 25

Between You and Me 26
After Reading Rilke's *Archaic Torso of Apollo* 28
Plenty 29
Wednesday 30
Almost a Happy Poem 31
Almost New Year 32

Jesus in the Temple with the Adulteress 35
Cana 36
Kinship 37
The Unbelief of Thomas 38
Veal Calf 40
Love Me 41
Morning 42
Old Crank 43
Always in October 44
Little Park 46
Those are pearls that were his eyes 47
Seed 48
One Small Place 49

One Family's Story   50
Muse   51
Athens, 400 BC   52
The Congo Free State, circa 1890   54
Small News Item in the Midst of War   55
Tonight   56
The Beekeeper in Rural Iraq   58
Sheridan and Pratt   59
Three Dreams in Three Colors   60
The Neighbor's Dog   62
and God will wipe away every tear from their eyes   63
Freelance Muse Looking for Roommate   64
Magnolia   65
In Their Company   66
Helen   67
Poem for Mary Rose O'Reilley   68
Meadow Lilies   69
On a Bench at Lincoln Park   70
My Jungle Cat   71
They Have Healed   72
Prodigal   74

SKY

Early evening in mid-February,
I looked up from the street of a city
still fresh with light
to see sparrows swooping together and unraveling
across sky that I became.

Now during tense afternoons
or dreamless nights,
part of me will remain
that shell-pink horizon
wild beings soared through.

My last hour on earth,
sky will breathe in me,
and wind-combed constellations of birds.
Let me remember the joy I felt
that moment in early spring
when I contained no boundaries.

NAMING

We have lost our ability to name.
We say *collateral damage, downsizing, factory farm.*
Error in judgment. Extraordinary rendition.
We say *sky,* but we don't mean it.
We say *antelope, owl,*
as if these words had power.
As if the names of animals hadn't long fled
back into animals,
where they pulse like black suns.

POETRY REMEMBERS

"Poetry ought to have a mother as well as a father."
—*Virginia Woolf*

I had a mother. The smell of earth after rain
mattered more to her than glory on battlefields.
Loneliness loved her. So did sorrow:
she befriended them both. *Men will tell you
I never existed*, she whispered to me once,
*but the little that you remember about me
will be enough.* Enough for what, I asked,
wanting only to stay in her arms
and bury my face in her hair,
which was fragrant and wild
as language, before language
became words.

AN EASTER POEM FOR CHRISTOPHER SMART

The eighteenth century poet grieved over cruelty to animals, referred to flowers as the poetry of Christ, and died in debtor's prison.

Christ's poetry blooms in your garden, Kit,
bluebells and hyacinth, crocus, pinks.
Soft paws of pussy willow climb new branches
as Jeoffry washes his face in a puddle of sun
and the lowliest toadstool sings.

Every ring has been removed
from the nose of every ox.
Bears baited in London theaters
roam mossy forests now, and slaughtered sows
praise God as sows should,
rolling on hairy backs and grunting joy.

This is the heaven I imagine for you,
Christopher. I believe that in Bedlam,
abandoned by all except one small cat,
you heard the tide of that great river
animals cross to come home—
sea turtles and parrots, work horses,
lambs. Vanquished or beaten,
turned into hair combs and glue,
they have risen with you
into nectar light.

Can this kingdom exist?
Let our longing create it.
Somewhere, you are reaching
toward your Savior's outstretched hand.

SHE ONLY WANTS TO WRITE

the thin keening of crickets this fragile May morning, and how the breath of her cat sleeping on a pillow behind her is a little cloud on the back of her neck. She knows if she links these two mysteries, she'll spin a bridge joining everything to everything, with her in the center, swaying on rope that braids itself as she casts down words, sinking full weight into each syllable without looking down.

TWO EXPERIMENTS AND AN ASIDE

A rhesus monkey will go without food for days
before giving her cage mate an electric shock
she knows is painful.
Researchers proved this in a West Coast laboratory.

Then there's that Harvard experiment
where students administered what they believed
dangerously high shock levels
to "slow learners"
who mock-writhed and jerked.

When imagining punishment for someone,
I have felt the voltage of hate
charge the length of my body.

Flesh becomes energy then:
its atomic structure alters,
heart tissue is damaged.

You don't feel it.

RED-TAILED FOX

Light-footed on diamond crust,
she leaves no trace of her swiftness,
blazes carnelian across the snowy miles
of a convicted man's dream.

Star shooting clean
in the mercy of sleep,
he will not remember her beauty,
she will bleed into something pale
as he surfaces,

clutching knuckles knifed raw
in a urine-stained cell,
no footprint of animal or god
on gun-gray cement,
no scent of the wild creature
that burst from his heart.

FIRST DAY AT BLACKLOCK NATURE SANCTUARY

For Marc

Who knew I'd start crying
when I kissed you goodbye yesterday?
You said *don't now* so tenderly
tears sting as I write, but this isn't
a sad poem. I saw a monarch drink calmly
from an iris this morning,
her folded wings one more petal.
I know that I love you like I know
rain is good, but it took
your sudden dearness to remind me
I'm a leaf floating on the surface
of that mystery.
Later, I watched darkening pine trees
shaken to wild grace by wind—
wind that touched everything.

MIGRATION

What if these shadows, brushed blue
across frozen lake,
tasted like dreams
to the geese gliding over them

What if these fir trees, leaning
into each other's secrets,
felt a questioning rather than wind
rippling their dusky bodies

What if this first day of March
I left my tight cluttered self
on the shore

and stepped into animal light,
into light sipped by rivers,
and kept walking

WILD SWAN OF NIMES
After the entitled abstract painting by Mary Abbott

Under whiteness of winter,
   green insists,
      pressing upward,
      splitting rock.

Islands of black ice
   keep cold secrets:
      owl's plummet,
      rabbit's freeze,

Around them sluice
   brown-muscled river,
      snow-melt and rain-swell
      gathering force.

I saw the swan's neck,
   his glass-dark beak
      in the shatter of leaves
        that for seconds was spring.

Then wild wings beat hard
   towards the rushing of water
      as branch became brushstroke
      and hid him in light.

IN THIS RAIN

When I was fifteen, I read in the paper how two teenage boys stoned a flamingo to death at Lincoln Park Zoo. Thirty years later, I think of this as I listen in my bedroom to early morning rain that begins quietly, like a shell held to the ear, but is steady and strong now. I have a sister I no longer talk to, a dead father I quarrel with nightly. He had large hands, my father, and tenderness towards animals, especially birds. Why are his eyes never blue in my dreams, why does he never laugh as he did when he was alive, laugh so hard he could never finish his joke, but would start to cry instead? She was alive when attendants found her, coral plumes scattered and smeared with blood. He did not understand cruelty any more than I do, although we were both capable of administering small, deliberate doses of it to each other. There are things I am not sure we are expected to forgive. There are others we must. I need to walk in this rain.

TAKING THE MASTER'S HAND

Some days, I can't do it.
I don't know how I ever did it.
I am sure I will never do it again—
write even one line of poetry.
If words were beads to be strung into necklaces,
my hands would be two stumps of ginger.
I sit on the bedroom floor and stare at sky,
then go for a walk around Lake Cedar,
reliving past mistakes.

After a rope-length of such days,
my future is a flat gray pond.
I leaf through an anthology of poems one morning
and read one by Tu Fu, a poet of the T'ang Dynasty.
His eight lines are not grand or difficult,
yet take me without effort to an old hermit's cottage
with words I know intimately: *sparrows, crickets, wine.*
I, too, have selected these words,
rolled them in my palms.
It was not impossible ...

I re-read Tu Fu's poem, marveling
how this modest rectangle of text
is a window leading me towards
ah, solid ground again—
                          sudden fragrance of pine—

SOMEONE IS BEATING A WOMAN

yet my coffee tastes delicious and my dreams were sweet as the slap of a man in charge who throws me against the wall and takes me but does not split my lip or break my nose, that is not sexy. It's sexy that lures, that country between tender and brutal: *don't go there*, we say when someone steps near our tinder, *don't go there*. It's not them we're warning. I've longed for years to stamp on the landmines I've buried, let the remains of my decency flutter like ash to the ground, but someone is beating a woman, punching her face, spit glitters, blood undelectable muddies the hands I imagine cupping my buttocks, my breasts, hands I created that want me that force

SEEL: TO STITCH CLOSED THE EYES (OF A FALCON) DURING TRAINING

What transparent thread, what sure and small fingers ignoring the pulse in a slender throat: fingers forced to hem yards of cloth by the lamp of one candle, transform rage into seamlessness. When his sky is sewn shut, the bird will fly in darkness, learn to obey one whose sons will make coats out of leopards and ash trays from the severed hands of silverbacks. Four hundred fresh elephant tusks decorating a reception hall in Brussels, a hill of bison skulls on which poses a white man who has personally shot twenty thousand head. Nations of animals gone, yet this moment stays with me, a serf girl of delicate build stitching shut the lids of a living creature for the pleasure of a man who owns her as well. Pain slipping into, then out of, trembling tissue.

CHINESE SEAHORSE
After the entitled painting by Marsden Hartley

I

The seahorse has large eyes, tiny hands, and a tail curled into itself. It has been painted into being and must endure the continual scrape of curious gazes. The seahorse wants to disappear into the soft underbelly of its own loneliness, but it can't, it is pinned to a canvas in a stark white museum where strangers dissect its brush strokes and tone.

II

Everywhere she looks, she sees the baby. His fists are the buds on a rose bush, his translucent toes are minnows in the aquarium of a pet store. She no longer goes to the supermarket, too many mothers and children, once hearing his sob in the next aisle, nearly collapsing with joy. These chilly February afternoons, she takes longer and longer walks with no destination. She wanders into churches to stare at stained glass. She drifts through museums.

III

The painting unnerves and enrages her, this alien creature with perfect fingers curled fetus-like inches away. Then she meets the eyes of the seahorse and their sorrow pierces something hard and dead. She stands in front of the painting for many minutes. When she steps into a wet evening, a small being's helplessness is sheltered inside her. She breathes in, for the first time in months, the goodness of rain.

COTTONWOODS

You know from their deeply grooved bark
they hold marvelous stories.
They are taller than oak trees
and sway and glitter through summer
like massive angels,
nearly brushing the clouds.
Can we doubt they are good?
Yet a neighbor used to say
with distinct disapproval
that "they'll grow anywhere."

Before this day ends, in some marketplace
where melons are stacked and ancients hum,
someone will toss a grenade.
A six-year-old who hates no one
will be diagnosed with leukemia.
A scrap of sapling will cling harder
to its patch of sandy earth, eager to bear
delicately scalloped leaves
shaped like what humans call hearts—

perfect to hold light
and give it back.

LAST DAY AT NORTH WOODS

This hour of hilltop and wind-shimmer,
acres of aspen glittering,
why should I have it?

The yellow butterfly
at my feet doesn't know.
She sips one garnet-ringed flower,
then another, ignoring
the two columns of boots in her path.

She doesn't know, and neither do I,
how soon after this brightness I will feel spite,
or swallow praise for a friend
because of a little envy.

DON'T DISAPPOINT THEM

Don't think you can squeeze in a lie
without leaving a thin trail of
slime on the page.

Never doubt your integrity
is at stake—
or that you will lose it.

You will stink with pretension.
You will fake epiphanies.
You will betray your own voice
and what you know to be true.

If you're lucky,
this will shame you. You'll try again,
remembering

that rain forgives
and pine trees listen.

FIRST STEP

Once, I assumed trees
could not remember.
If someone had told me stars mourn
when a member of their constellation dies,
I would have thought it a metaphor.
My ignorance is vast.
But at its heart
lies a small shrine,
the prayer mat waiting—

So I must learn to listen to stone;
to cup flame, stumbling forward a little,
when after centuries of my kind's savagery
I meet an animal's eyes
and they darken with love.

MEETING SOPHIA

jolts me into sun diamonds and crunching snow
as we turn round and around, myself attempting
to unravel her leash from my knees as she
follows me eagerly with wet nose
and lapping tongue. Sophia!
who sensed, on this winter path, my longing
and leapt toward it, a sleek muscle of joy
that nearly knocked me down,
all kisses and corn silk-soft ears and a name
that means Wisdom, a name
that is not wasted on this animal
whose owner, an elderly man wearing woolen ear flaps,
is crying, *Sophia, have some manners, Sophia,*
in a charmingly accented voice that Sophia
wisely ignores, continuing to kiss
and kiss this strange woman who smelled like
sadness a moment ago, this woman
who is now laughing.

GREAT, GREY / SISTERLY SHAPE

Something large and soft and rounded rising out of sea and mist. Not frightening, but knowable? Breaching, then descending, taking part of me with her. Our entire history a chain of myths we create only to understand too late or not at all. What shape, childhood? Is it closer to ocean? All language metaphor, but not all experience stretched or amputated into language. Flowing instead into shapes that are not words: massive, gentle. Breaching, then descending.

A GOOD THING

You can stick him in a highchair under hot lights
until he grins for the camera.
Or put him in a boxing ring and make him throw punches.
You can even strap him inside a rocket
and blast it towards space.
                                    He'll forgive you.
You can test cleaning products on her skin,
or inject her with any number of diseases.
You can break her vertebrae, glue it together.
She'll forgive you.
                        She'll be grateful
if you visit the cell where she's been dumped.
If her brain is shrieking, you won't hear it.
And that's a good thing, friend; a good thing
neither of us can hear the long red animal scream
wrapping itself around our planet.

ON WASHINGTON AVENUE BRIDGE

On Washington Avenue Bridge,
mist rises from the Mississippi
like white smoke from many fires.

We have poisoned our planet, starved her,
done our best to defile her,
but look—the river this January morning
is wide and still,
steam melting like sacrifice
into brilliant blue air.

High above the Mississippi,
crows with centuries of fury caught
deep in their throats
slice cold with slow wings.

Better off without you,
they scream, their anger
fitting, and harsh,
and sometimes lost utterly
in rising columns of mist.

HER HEAVEN

Let her wake
to a rough tongue

cherishing
the length of her;

to cloud-warmth
of milk and fur,

no memory
of metal or blood.

Two bodies,
one dream.

Little star-breath
drifting through night.

BETWEEN YOU AND ME

Don't you love that breathlessness before dusk
when trees are crisp and black against December?
Less a fragment of late afternoon
than a way of seeing, each roof and branch
pressed flat against lambent sky.

I used to believe I knew myself.
I used to believe I was separate
from what broke in waves around me.
Lately, I have sensed a different way
of moving through days—
something softer and slower, like pushing gently
through clouds and water, only you, too,
are the clouds and the water,
the green memory of someone you loved
and the distance and the grief.

It's all right if you don't understand.
It's all right if you want a life
as polished and precise
as one of those twigs stenciled on twilight.

But have you ever walked home at noon or at dusk,
in winter or in summer, and not remembered
how you found your way back?
And when you realized you had not been
you, but all that you walked on, and by,
and through, weren't you happier for it?
Couldn't you almost name who you were?

AFTER READING RILKE'S
ARCHAIC TORSO OF APOLLO

A great poem
shatters what I am
into flakes flying everywhere.

When the whirlwind subsides
and gravity
takes hold,

I am newborn,
falling flawlessly
into myself again.

PLENTY

I have your sausage-thick fingers, Dad,
your bad singing voice,
your will to keep old wounds open.
I smell your stubbornness in my sweat.
As a child, I never knew what to say to you.
Now I shout at you in half-lit dreams
when I can wrench syllables from shaking lips.
You gaze back, unmoved.
But I remember an awkward bear hug you gave me,
a morning when I was nineteen
and just the two of us drank coffee
in a kitchen's milky light.
Tell me the dead understand their lives
better than the living.
Tell me that I, who for thirty-eight years
never spoke back,
could say something today
to make your Swedish-blue eyes
alive with affection—
not for a stranger's child,
or the daughter you loved—
but for me,
who has cursed and raged and hoarded
your every tenderness.

WEDNESDAY

On the bus, workday mornings, I watch girls
in tall boots and high heels step past the driver.
They smooth skirts before sitting down
and opening sleek little phones:
earnest and beautiful enough,
these young women whose cheekbones
are stroked by long fingers of sun,
to soften anyone's heart.
Today, one in blue studies a tiny computer screen
and touches what looks like
a brand new pearl barrette
chosen seriously at Macy's.

I remember when a hair ornament
meant that much to me. I sit in gym shoes,
holding my lunch and a paperback of poems,
neither wistful nor bitter. Yet I look at this girl,
who may or may not know how
lovely she is, and I think about my life,
and suddenly tears sting.

ALMOST A HAPPY POEM

I am clamoring out of
thick dreams when
a thump and a chirrup
tell me she has landed.
She leaps neatly over
my face, then navigates
with sure feet
towards the crescent
of warm bed
waiting. I stroke her
black coat, feeling
the bloom of her purr
intensify, as if
her small body contained
a garden throbbing
with throats and wings.
Her wet nose pushes
bossily against any skin
it can find,
and when she
nests her entire head
in the cup of my palm,
her trust is so
complete, my heart
breaks a little.

ALMOST NEW YEAR

In snow, along railroad tracks, perhaps
twenty crows. They flew out of a folktale
into this December morning, bringing their
shining black truth with them.
Tonight, they'll collect in tall branches,
so in violet air winter trees will seem laden
with forbidden fruit.
                                      I hurt two good women
this past year. Both have forgiven me.
And just now, startled into flight,
three blackbirds revealed what was still possible.
Their wings, like torn pieces of night,
held every color,
bore dark, shining gifts towards sky.

JESUS IN THE TEMPLE WITH THE ADULTERESS
John 8:1-11

What were you thinking
when you sketched figures in dust

as if time were a luxury
like laughter, or scented oil,

as if the elders' red eyes
did not sear your back,

as if you did not feel the woman's terror
enormous inside you.

You did not know her fate.

You did not know, until you spoke,
what words would come,

or guess, until the mob retreated
into the streets of that narrow town

and you were alone with her,
how intimate this moment.

She lifted her gaze.
You almost could not look.

CANA

The miracle was not necessary.
No servant writhed with devils,
no child lay dying.
Mary simply wanted to spare a young couple
the shame of running out of wine
at their own wedding.

For this?
Jesus asked his mother.
She did not say yes,

but what light on her face
as she saw her son ripen that day
from perfection
to a man who spilled his divinity
into six stone urns,
and drank it freely with others.

KINSHIP

"He took the blind man by the hand ... Putting spittle on his eyes he laid his hands on him and asked, 'Do you see anything?' Looking up, he replied, 'I see people looking like trees and walking.'"
—Mark 8:24

I, too, have seen elms and poplars
against December,
have imagined their poses as wonder,
or longing, or joy.

Their roots suckled life,
their stems pushed sunward
ages before we discovered fire,
invented sin.

A healer through whose rib cage
tide and gale rippled
would have felt this,
might have wanted to give a blind man
vision before sight—

a world where trees walked like men,
so that after reality dimmed understanding,
that man could not press his palm
against the trunk of a cypress
without a quickening.
A kinship.

THE UNBELIEF OF THOMAS
John 20:25

Dipping three fingers into the warm bath
of wound was not, after all, enough.
The moment melted to color and shame,
someone's soft gasp
as he withdrew his hand.

Had he, Thomas, done that?
Dreams of crouching in caves,
running naked through buckling streets,
were as real as that room where strips of sunset
kindled exhausted but joyful faces.
Thomas could barely breathe air
so thick with expectation.
Little food, little sleep,
sure he was being followed.

Yet smiles behind those barred doors,
laughter even, "he is coming, be patient."
Who were these men whose odor and sweat
he once knew? Only *he* seemed the same
when Thomas heard his name spoken quietly
and turned—

Little food, little sleep.
Unsurprised when the dried roots of olive trees
licked his ankles like fire.
Faces hurt him with their brightness,
and eyes, he did not look at eyes,
since meeting his teacher's and nearly slipping
down, down into light.

VEAL CALF

He imagines more than we know,
this dreamy newborn.
No notion of profit or cruelty
in his milky brain.
Brown eyes sing creation
as the psalmist envisioned.

Quick, mother,
with a sand-rough tongue
fill the hills and valleys
of your baby with love.

LOVE ME

> "… [he called] creatures, no matter how small, by the name of brother or sister, because he knew they had the same source as himself."
> —Bonaventure, *The Life of St. Francis*

Do we frighten angels
with our ugliness?—
we who divide creation between
beautiful and not?
The shock of a spider's eyes
opens darkness in me
that swallows sky.
Was that cave in Francis, too?
Did he enter it, trembling,
again and again, until
tiny legs exploring his flesh
seemed delicate music?
I have hated and killed
so many small lives.
Yet I sing to the world,
love me, love me.

MORNING

*"I could not cure myself of praying to a
God I no longer believed in."*
—Joanna Macy

But I do believe. He knows that.
I talk to him as I drink coffee in the morning.
I give him angels.
When I wake in darkness, severed
from myself and from him,
he knows my terror.
He allows me to pray
him back into being.

OLD CRANK

She walked the streets of her suburb, an old crank who considered herself a failure. Down littered bike paths she trudged, jarred by cyclists who screamed "on your left!" so loudly she thought her heart would jump out of her chest. One day, it did. She bent to retrieve it, but what she thought would be light shocked her back with its weight. How heavy her heart was!—and white, like sun-baked stone. Holding it solemnly with both hands, she gave it a shy lick: salty. If she boiled this old heart in water, would it dissolve? That would be one way to incorporate it into her body again. She did not want to do this. There was a small forest preserve nearby where she had once seen three deer at sunset. She would leave her heart in the open for deer to lick and nibble. What a comfort to know she would never realize when it disappeared completely.

ALWAYS IN OCTOBER

The man in the blue work shirt
asleep on the train this morning,
light filling the hollow of his throat,

and the brightness I waded through
on my lunch hour,
wave after wave of yellow leaves,
traced and cut out, it seemed,
by children in love with stars—

I don't need to tell you.
Some days a thread's tossed
and I catch it, travel with confidence
among strangers, trust the orange moon
rising between buildings
knows every valley and curve inside me.

Some days I can almost articulate
what flows beneath autumn.
You remember that hour
bare branches were fingers
you wanted to touch.

Tonight, as I walked home in a neighborhood
where fear litters street corners,
a boy smiled at me for no reason.
And the evening was soft,
it slid past me like a beautiful animal,
and my body was light and sure.

LITTLE PARK

What will we do with this little park
on the edge of a city,
this brave scrap of green?
Orange-tipped blackbirds
believe it's their kingdom.
So does that goose waddling by
pensively as a scholar.
Ducks gabbing about politics
don't seem to mind the plastic bottles
bobbing alongside them,
and look at the white heron
torn from a myth,
lovely and motionless
on the spray-painted pier!

Who saw the humans
smash their gazebo into pieces last night?
What will we do with this robin,
puffing his chest out
and daring the world?

THOSE ARE PEARLS THAT WERE HIS EYES

Coral clings to my heart.
Somewhere rain falls through truisms.
A wounded otter, didn't he ramble
down halls of my childhood,
and did a balmy fox burst out of a dream once
to tell me something important?
God, I have grown to love
this lulling and rocking, strange memories
drifting up through green darkness
like flecks of light descending the wrong way ...
But my eyes. Where are my eyes?

SEED

Wings over frozen shore. What door slipped open so she drifts above unborn rivers, a sickle of beach where a woman and child sleep, curled in the arc of a silver wolf who sleeps with them? Flower inside of flower, dreaming deep inside her, until she floats upward, breaks into white light of morning.

ONE SMALL PLACE

My mother believed Eden was the whole earth.
Then we sinned, and "our intellect darkened."
That phrase seduced me as a child:
I pictured tracts of water and land
suddenly dimmed, like sky before storm.

Tonight, I sit on a bench
watching a couple push their children on swings:
the mother, their toddler,
the father, their baby,
who is whooping and gurgling,
his hair bright as duckling's down.

A boy of about fourteen
is swinging too, as high as he can,
no friends around to witness this lapse of cool.

I hear we're due for a storm.
I think it will be a terrible one.
You would never guess it from the gold
lingering in this park,
wind combing cottonwoods
until they swell like distant surf.

ONE FAMILY'S STORY
Genesis 19

Her body shook from the explosions,
hot wind and horror sang in her ears.
She looked back at what had been home,
not prudent like her husband
who did not waste a glance on her cinder.
An expedient man. Quick to choose,
years earlier, the greenest pastureland
when he and his herdsman brother parted ways,
but ingratiating when it served—
offering, in those days before catastrophe,
his own daughters to drunken thugs,
rather than risk insult to guests
who could help him escape.
He made forgetting an art,
but could never erase his wife's last soft cry,
or the moans of his two girls,
pressed against him on the cave's floor
that evening the sheets of fire
finally stopped raining,
and the three of them drank a calfskin of wine
to celebrate their deliverance.

MUSE

"Every angel is terrible."
—Rilke

When I was nineteen and read "Fern Hill"
for the first time, I imagined the author
luminous as he composed the poem.

Years later, I read Thomas's letters:
the vulgarities he used to describe women,
his disgust over ordinary villagers.

Dylan Thomas, of blackouts and incoherent brawls,
who died dissipated and fat. The man
poetry coursed through like white flame.

It's enough to make me believe she *does* exist,
pitching her tent randomly,
indifferent to holocausts she leaves behind.

ATHENS, 400 BC

We don't know whose family gained most
from the match, or how keenly
her heart sank when she first saw him,

only that Socrates' wife married him
when he was well into middle age,
boasting a pot belly and an aversion to bathing.

Three sons she bore the philosopher,
all under the age of twelve
when he sipped the hemlock,

which means, though we think of her
as a nagging fifty-year-old,
she, too, must have been young.

"A shrew," historians (male, upper-class)
assure us, since Plato notes in his Dialogues
how she harpied his beloved teacher

who strolls now, in a clean robe,
through a glen of oak trees
with a flock of prep school boys.

Meanwhile, Xanthippe
(that is her name)
beats laundry against rocks.

Southeast of the city, slave-worked silver mines
that keep this democracy thriving
hum with horror.

THE CONGO FREE STATE, CIRCA 1890

He looks into our faces with irony
so unnerving, I do not at first notice
the stumps that were arms.

The caption does not explain
his mutilation or the shock
of a slightly raised eyebrow.

He spoke back to a white man.
Starved, he smuggled a piece of meat
or paid twice for a Belgian's mistake.

Tonight he is honored. Tonight
Debussy settles soft on our shoulders
as we sip chilled wine
and murmur among photographs.

This man who could not
feed himself
studies us like God.

SMALL NEWS ITEM IN THE MIDST OF WAR

It could be chance that out of
our own darkness
and the world's,
out of sleep
and that hour before dawn,
the first sound we hear,
if we are lucky enough
to live where they make their homes,
is the liquid questioning of a bird,
testing the day's reality with her song.

And maybe the bubbles that cluster
like clear beads on stems in vases
are chance too, and the elaborate feathers
of ice that form on windows in winter.
Beauty could be an accident.

So I must not make too much
of the bird I read about
who built her nest from the scrap
of detonated land mines:

who absolves, every morning,
the wreckage of a greenless field
with notes that sound beautiful.

TONIGHT

In memory of Jiří Orten, 1919 - 1941

I wanted to make something
beautiful for you, reader,
to arrange words on a page
as if they were pure yellow leaves
plucked from smoky October.
But today a woman told me
a story about a man:
told me how decades ago, in a granite city,
he was dragged by a car,
then left at a hospital where doctors
refused to admit him
because he was Jewish.
I don't know if those doctors, long dead,
are free from nightmares tonight.
Or how long, denied morphine,
it took for the man to die.

I am thinking of what a saint said
about a different crucifixion: that its mystery
was reserved for the future.
Francis knew time was fluid, but like the rest of us,
flinched from pain.
In middle age, before his eyes were cauterized,
he asked the fire to be kind.

Tonight, I believe
those blue flames listened. I believe
if we pray hard enough,
rivers can flow backward.

He was an artist, the woman told me,
and he was young.
Let us kneel, tonight, beside his ruined body.
Let us stay with him.

THE BEEKEEPER IN RURAL IRAQ

I want to lift these wet lilacs into my arms
and love them as he would,
bowing my face into their heaven.

I want his brown hands, callused and tapered,
to become my own, I want
to touch this rain-heavy sweetness

as he touches the mossy bellies of his bees
who cluster on his unprotected flesh
and do not sting.

He tells the reporter that when he was young,
his whole country smelled of flowers.
He tells of bees' generosity,

how they will share their honey with you
"if you are not greedy."
I want to love these wet Minnesota lilacs

as he would, in his land of paved-over orchards
and bombed mosques: cradling the blossoms
like children, crooning a little.

SHERIDAN AND PRATT

Outside the convenience store in early evening,
I stare at the large man wobbling towards me
on a rusty bike he manages with one hand
while the other cups something against his breast.

He stutters *hello ma'am*,
asks if I'll hold the kitten he found
under a parked car two blocks away.
His big hands shake as he gives her to me.

I'm speechless for the slender purr,
the lost star on one silky foot.

He comes out of the store with cat food, milk,
a slow man with a hesitant smile,
thumbnails bigger than her paws.

After he's pocketed her and nosed his bike into traffic
(plastic bag swinging from handle bars),
my eyes follow them
until there's only taillights and dusk.

THREE DREAMS IN THREE COLORS

Red

I hate pain and humiliation, I said.
She said she did, too. She was kind.
You meet kind people in all professions.
We were in an alley outside the sex shop.
She told me what a man did to a woman
with her back arched, in the position he requested.
"But most men aren't like that."

Later, on the other side of town,
I knew I would not go back there
either to work or to spy.
They were hosing down trees in the plaza.
I was not allowed to help wash off the blood.

Black

I stood on a cliff and looked down into sea
after the girl's murder. Or maybe before.
We had sat on a wall together. I could have warned her.
She was dark-haired, rather pretty
and rather spoiled.
                        The island had right angles
everywhere, alleys ending at canals,
streets perpendicular to ocean.

I didn't hate the girl. Why didn't I tell her
of their plans? So many directions
emptying into water.

There are no corners in water.

Silver
There was a hill, of course,
with a house at the top—
marble, with pillars and a dome.
The vestibule was moonlit,
gleaming shafts I could walk through.
I wanted to stay,
explore deeper rooms,
but a woman said terrible things had happened here.

I knew she was right.
Still it was beautiful, this place
where stone slept with rage.

THE NEIGHBOR'S DOG

She knew when I turned
from Willow to Allen,
walking home from the train station
to visit my mother.

She let out cries for a long lost friend,
lay on her back, legs tangled in rope,
while I stroked matted ears,
pressed my palm on the soft concave of her belly.

Sometimes children played in the yard.
She ran with them across trampled grass
until the line jerked her back.

The owners said she turned mean,
jumped the fence one night
dragging rope behind her.

I remember her contentment
in a patch of sun one frigid afternoon,
the ridges of her backbone as I petted her.

She would have forgiven almost anything.

AND GOD WILL WIPE AWAY EVERY TEAR FROM THEIR EYES

At its center,
the circle inverts:
the food chain collapses,
the lion eats straw.
Yet tears are not reversed,
but are *wiped away*.
So necessary to me, that God
who lets tears fall.
Who touches a quail's grief
with his own hand.

FREELANCE MUSE LOOKING FOR ROOMMATE

who values my company. Can't help with food, rent or utilities. Cats preferred. I also like Renaissance music and a window. Don't tell me not to read your poems over your shoulder, and don't mind if I laugh at them. I won't be early or often. When I do drop in, I'll bring the red and black snowflake mitten you lost when you were four, or the smell of Raid and ancient linoleum from your first apartment in the city. The room where you learned loneliness.

MAGNOLIA

The bare shrub
unnoticed by me
in February

has snow clumps
still clinging to it
in late March

which, when examined,
are plump,
purple-veined
buds.

A day later,
I blink:
it appears

some unnecessary stars
fell quietly
from last night's
sky,

and settled lightly
lightly
among shivering
branches.

IN THEIR COMPANY

My old tabby has left the comfort of his basket
and climbed with shaky, arthritic legs
up three plastic steps to the bed,
hoisting his hind quarters onto the blanket,
then settling himself carefully.
His sister, whose black fur is flecked white,
already rests on the pillow beside me.
She does not hiss at her former nemesis,
but is calm and watches me, as he does,
with great dark eyes.

I thought this sadness was too deep
to be shared with anyone,
even the man in the next room,
yet these two have found their way
to this low, starless place
no human willingly enters.
They will not let me be alone here.

HELEN

You died in the month of deepest blue—
September,
when leaf clusters ripen to yellow,
and afternoons throb still with summer.

Born in a Midwestern frost,
a grim town of steel and limestone
forged the little girl I remember from a photograph.
She stands sternly by a horse at seven,
this motherless child, with eyes
that will tolerate only truth.

Years later, you gave so easily to me
gifts *you* never received:
guardian angels, clouds that were little lambs.

You died in the month
of deepest skies, lushest noons.
The dull gleam of metal,
the quiet of hospital machines stopped
from pump and drone
was not your death.

September opened
and took you seamlessly.

POEM FOR MARY ROSE O'REILLEY
Teacher, poet, wild animal rehabilitator

The morning you lectured on Descartes,
crows collected on branches
outside your classroom:

collected by dozens
and hurled into February's cold
their harsh syllable.

Caws beat against glass,
your hall rained cacophony.
The theories of a dead philosopher

who had animals whipped and nailed
for the thrill of a little knowledge
were out-shouted that day

by riotous grackles. How they exulted!—
drowning idea, severed from flesh,
with raw song.

MEADOW LILIES

Each fluted white body
bears a stain of magenta
like a bright splash of pain.

Imagine your secret
exposed
to any grazing eye.

Now think
if it were
beautiful.

ON A BENCH AT LINCOLN PARK

I ask the woman in sweatpants
if her dog is friendly,
and we get to talking.
They wouldn't tell her at the shelter
what was done to him,
but when she first brought him home,
he crouched under the bed without eating
for three days.

He's a Doberman,
with clipped ears, a docked tail,
and such numinous brown eyes
I lay my face against his side,
which is warm with sun.

These deep simple necessities
by which life renews itself.
We never earn them, do we?

In early spring light,
he lets me hold him
for a long time.

MY JUNGLE CAT

Nightly, I build a house of remorse
and people it with indifferent ghosts.

On a branch high above guilt,
she watches.

Sometimes she yawns, swallowing
all my dark rooms.

Sometimes I wake fearless
from the red flower of her throat.

THEY HAVE HEALED

They have healed the wound of my people
lightly saying peace
when there is no peace.

Words she copied on an envelope in a chapel
where sun blessed cobalt and ruby.
No prophet's or saint's name under the message.
Yet someone had sewn the letters,
hung the banner.

Say sky where there is no sky.
Say garden where there is no garden.

Once on an icy corner,
a man buttoned her coat as if she were a child
and tied her scarf with bare hands.
She should have unfolded herself to him.
She didn't know how.

Does not know how this late hour,
begging an imaginary Father for light,
repeating the words she wrote down today,
saying *peace* when there is no peace,
remembering those weather-roughened hands
saying *trust*.

PRODIGAL

In the cardiology waiting room, I glance away
from the news program a cluster of us watch
and wander toward an aquarium at the other end.
In clear water, fish tremble like exotic cut-outs,
flashing hot violet and chartreuse
for rows of empty chairs.

They remind me how prodigal beauty is.
Think of sunflowers offering themselves
at the edges of freeways, never caring
if they're prized.
Beauty seems the opposite to me of evil,
which weighs advantages expertly
and wastes nothing—
neither a mother's terror, nor a child's trust,
nor the gold fillings of the dead.

Beauty throws away acres
of pear blossom and burnished maple
season after season, never learning
to be prudent, yet saving my heart
again and again—
my stapled-together heart
that refuses to remain open.

But look at the opalescent
bodies of these fish.
When they press silver noses against glass,
their gazes are tender.

Notes

Someone is beating a woman is the title and first line of a poem by Andrei Voznesensky.

The italicized definition of "seel" is from *Webster's New Universal Unabridged Dictionary*.

Great, grey / sisterly shape is from Paul Celan's poem, "Alchemical."

and God will wipe away every tear from their eyes —Revelation 7:17.

Those are pearls that were his eyes —from *The Tempest*.

The italicized lines in "On a Bench at Lincoln Park" are from Rilke's *Letters to a Young Poet*.

The italicized lines in "They Have Healed" are from *Isaiah*.

www.ingramcontent.com/pod-product-compliance
Lightning Source LLC
Chambersburg PA
CBHW031208090426
42736CB00009B/824